Contents

GW00359518

Acknowledgements
The publishers would like to thank
Karakal for their photographic
contribution to this book.

Photographs on the outside covers
courtesy of Sporting Pictures (UK) Ltd.
All other photographs by Stephen Line.
Thanks to Angus Kirkland for taking part
in the demonstrations.
Thanks to Brighton Squash Club for
providing the relevant facilities.
Illustrations by Margaret Jones.

Note Throughout the book players
and officials are referred to individually
as 'he'. This should, of course, be taken
to mean 'he or she' where appropriate.
Similarly, the instructions in the text
are geared towards right-handed
players; left-handers should simply
reverse these instructions.

Introduction

Squash, or to give the game its full title,
squash rackets has grown at a remarkably rapid rate, not only because it is
fun, induces competitiveness, aids fit-
ness and stimulates social activity – but
also because those that try it find it easy
to learn.

However, whether you are a begin-
ner or a more experienced player, to get
more fun from, and to become more
proficient at the game, some guidance
and advice is essential. The best form of
this is of course individual coaching
from a qualified coach.

This book will provide you with the
ideas to practise and put into your
game which will take you to the next
level, or if you are lucky enough to
receive regular coaching it will serve to
remind you of the things you will learn
there.

The advice on play in this book was
written by the late Sam Jagger who
coached squash at Lancing College for
27 years.

Note

The scoring described in this book is
the International system. There is also
a system used in North America
whereby games are 15-up, and every
point is scored, i.e. a player serving
hand-out (*see* page 3) concedes a point
as well as the service. The men's profes-
sional game also sometimes plays
15-up (point-a-rally).

The game

The game of squash is played between two players. The ball is served by one player, from a service box, on to the front wall above the cut line, so that on its rebound it falls into the opposite back quarter of the court bounded by the half-court line and the short line.

The server is known as 'hand-in' and the receiver as 'hand-out'.

Hand-out may then either volley the ball or hit the ball after it has bounced once on the floor. In either case, he plays the ball to the front wall either directly or by way of a side or back wall, and the server then receives and returns it similarly. Play goes on until a player fails to make a good return, when his opponent scores a point (if hand-in) or takes over the service (if hand-out). Only the server can score points.

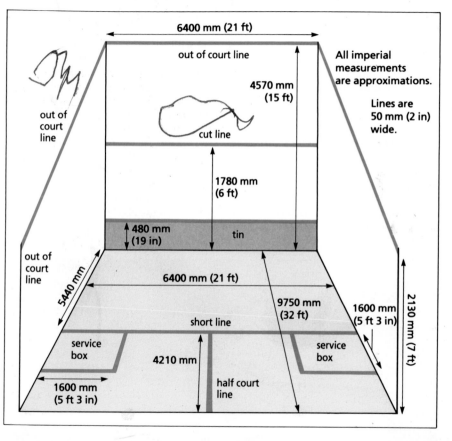

Fig. 1 Dimensions of the court ▶

3

A return is 'good' so long as:

- the ball remains within the boundaries of the court
- the ball hits the front wall above the 'tin' before it touches the floor
- the ball does not bounce on the floor more than once before it is returned.

A marker controls matches, but usually a referee is appointed as well. The latter is in overall control and makes all decisions covering lets, the award of points and appeals against calls of the marker by either player. Where there is only one official he must act in both capacities.

The court

The walls of the court should be white or near white. The size of the court is standard and all floor and wall dimensions are measured from the junction of the floor and walls. Lines are painted red and should be 50 mm (2 in) wide, whether on the floor or walls of the court. The 'tin' consists of a plywood or metal sheet extending right across the front wall, surmounted by a strip of wood, known as the board, painted red. The height to the top of this board is 480 mm (19 in) from the floor.

Equipment

Clothing

The usual clothing for men is shorts, white squash shoes (with soles that do not mark the floor) and a white or pastel short-sleeved shirt. Women normally wear a white or pastel blouse or shirt with a short skirt or shorts.

The racket

The head and shaft of the racket are usually made of graphite, carbon fibre or aluminium. It is strung with gut, nylon or similar material, and must not weigh more than 255 g (9 oz). There may be some 'whip' in the shaft and the grip may be of any suitable material – e.g. leather, rubber or towelling. A towel grip is very popular as it helps to absorb perspiration. The most suitable racket is usually chosen by 'feel', but the dimensions of the racket shown in the illustration to the right (fig. 2) are maximum and should not be exceeded.

◀ *Squash shoe*

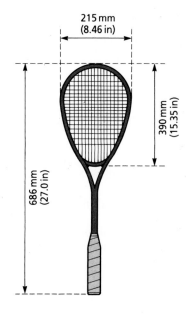

▲ *Fig. 2 Squash racket and its dimensions*

The ball

The rubber ball is small and round with an even matt surface and finish. It is obtainable in varying speeds to suit the ability of the player and/or the temperature of the court. These speeds are indicated by a coloured dot: yellow (very slow, used by most regular players), white (slow), red (medium) and blue (fast).

The size is shown in the photograph below and it should be between 23.5 g and 24.4 g in weight. Balls must pass the testing committee of the Squash Rackets Association and, if they comply with the specifications laid down, they may bear the standard SRA mark.

▲ *Squash ball and its dimensions*

Service

The right to serve first is decided by the spin of a racket and the server may serve from either service box.

X wins the toss and serves. Y returns the ball and from then it is struck alternately until X either wins a point or loses the service. X continues to score points as long as he continues to win rallies while serving. If X puts the ball out of court, into the tin or board, serves a fault or is beaten by Y's return, Y then becomes the server and so on throughout the match.

For the initial service of each game or 'hand' the server may serve from either box, but after scoring a point he serves from the other box and then from each box alternately as long as he remains hand-in.

If hand-in serves from the wrong box and his opponent takes the service, there is no penalty and the service counts as if it had been made from the correct box. His opponent may demand the service to be re-taken from the correct box, provided he has not returned or attempted to return the service.

Points are scored by hand-in when his opponent fails to make a good return.

If hand-in serves from the right-hand service box, he may take up the position shown in the left-hand photograph on the page opposite, ready to deliver a forehand service. The backhand stroke may also be used from this service box.

A service from the left-hand court may also be served either forehand or backhand but the following points must be observed to make a correct service.

● Stand with one foot or both feet touching the floor completely within the service box.
● Throw the ball from the hand into the air.
● Serve the ball on to the front wall above the cut line so that on its return, unless volleyed, it would fall on the floor in the quarter court nearest the back wall and opposite to the service box from which the service has been delivered (fig. 3).

◀ *Fig. 3 The service*

Service faults

Note When a fault is served, the right to serve is lost.

(1) It is a foot-fault unless the server has at least one foot in contact with the floor, within the service box, at the moment of striking the ball: no part of this qualifying foot may be touching a line, the wall or the floor outside the box, though the other foot may be anywhere inside or outside the box (*see* photograph far right).

(2) It is a fault if the ball is served under the front wall on or below the 'cut' line.

(3) It is a fault if the ball first touches the floor on the half-court line or in the half court from which the service is delivered.

(4) It is a fault if the ball first touches the floor on or in front of the short line, i.e. if it drops short of the service court.

(5) It is a fault if the server fails to hit the ball correctly (termed 'not up').

(6) It is a fault if the server serves the ball out of court.

(7) It is a fault if the ball strikes another wall before the front wall.

▲ *Service on forehand from right-hand service box*

▲ *Foot-fault*

(8) It is a fault if the ball touches the server or anything he wears or carries before it has bounced twice.

Serving hand-out

Server serves his hand-out and loses the service:

● if he fails to hit the ball correctly or the ball does not at least carry to the front wall above the tin
● if he serves the ball out of court
● if the ball strikes another wall before the front wall
● if the ball touches the server or anything he wears or carries before it has bounced twice.

Appeals to referee

Hand-in may appeal against the marker's call of 'fault', 'foot-fault', 'out', 'down' or 'not up'. Hand-out may appeal against the marker's failure to make any of these calls. In the latter case he should play the ball and only appeal if he loses the subsequent rally.

Return and subsequent play

After the service is delivered, play should be continuous as far as possible. Bad light or other circumstances beyond the players' control may stop play. If play is resumed the same day, the match shall continue with the score as it was when play ceased, but if it is resumed the next or a subsequent day, the score shall stand unless both players agree to start the match again.

Good return

A return is good if the ball, before it has bounced twice on the floor, is returned by the striker on to the front wall above the board, without touching the floor or any part of the striker's body or clothing, provided the ball is not hit twice or out of court.

Winning the rally

A player wins the rally:

● when his opponent serves his hand-out

● if his opponent fails to made a good return of the ball in play

● if the ball touches the striker's opponent or anything he wears or carries, except in those cases otherwise provided for under 'obstructions'.

Hand-in scores a point if he wins the rally.

Hand-out gains the service if he wins the rally.

Squash Rackets Association
Westpoint
33–34 Warple Way
Acton
London
W3 0RQ

tel   **0181 746 1616**

Scoring

A match consists of the best of five games, each game being of 9-up. The player first winning nine points wins the game, except that, if the score is called eight-all for the first time, hand-out may, if he chooses, before the next service is delivered, set the game to two. In this case, the player who first scores two points wins the game.

These two points do not have to be scored consecutively. Hand-out must in either case clearly indicate his choice to the marker, if any, and to his opponent, by saying either 'Set one' or 'Set two'.

The score does not go beyond ten. Thus, in the case of 'Set one' one player will win the game 9–8, and in the case of 'Set two' one player will win it 10–9 or 10–8.

The marker

The game is controlled by the marker, who calls the play and score. The server's score is called first.

If during play the marker calls 'Not up', 'Out' or 'Down', the rally must stop and if his decision is altered on appeal a 'let' is allowed, unless the referee decrees that the marker has called 'Not up', 'Out' or 'Down' to an undoubted winning shot which was in fact correct, in which case he may award the stroke accordingly.

When no referee is appointed the marker exercises all the powers of the referee.

Referees

A referee may be appointed and, if so, all appeals are directed to him.

The decision of the referee is final.

Let

A let is an undecided stroke, and the service or rally in respect of which a let is allowed does not count and the service is taken again from the same box.

Keeping out of opponent's way

A player must do all he can to give his opponent a clear and fair view of the ball in play and give him room to play his stroke. A player must always leave his opponent as far as possible free to play the ball to any part of the front wall or to either side wall near the front wall.

If in the opinion of the referee there is unnecessary interference with the striker, 'Stop' is called. Play stops at once and a stroke is awarded to the player interfered with.

Unnecessary crowding constitutes obstruction, even if the player is not actually prevented from reaching or playing the ball.

Is it a let or a stroke?

If a fair ball, after hitting the front wall and before being played again, touches a player or anything he wears or carries before touching the floor twice, the touched player loses the stroke.

If a ball is struck as a good return and it hits the striker's opponent or anything he wears or carries before it rea-

▲ *Fig. 4 Blue player loses stroke*

ches the front wall, it is a stroke to the striker if the ball would have reached the front wall directly, unless the striker had 'turned' on the ball, or has already played and missed.

If a ball is struck as a good return, but would have hit either side wall first, it is a let. Similarly if a good return has already hit the side wall on its way to

▲ Fig. 5 Unnecessary obstruction: red
player loses stroke

Fig. 6 Top centre *Red player loses stroke*

Fig. 7 Top right *Red player loses stroke*

the front wall, it is also a let, unless an
undoubted winning shot has been
intercepted, in which case a stroke is
awarded.

If a ball would not have made a good
return, the striker shall lose the stroke.
Other cases in which a let is allowed are
detailed in World Squash Federation
rule 13.

▲ Fig. 8 Let

▲ Fig. 9 Blue player loses stroke

Strokes

Grip

The best method for gripping the racket is to shake hands with the handle, forming a 'V' between the thumb and forefinger, presenting the racket with an open face as shown in the photographs on the right. Many players have developed their own variations on this, and provided a player has a grip which is comfortable and enables him to play the full range of forehand and backhand strokes successfully, then that particular grip is correct for him.

Do not grip the racket tightly. Every muscle of your body should be relaxed when you position yourself ready to strike the ball. This is even true of the fingers that grip the racket. Only when you strike the ball does your grip tighten.

▲ *Grip, from above*

Grip, from the side ▶

12

The swing of the racket

A good striking technique is as important in squash as it is in either golf or tennis. It is an advantage to those taking up the game to try to form an effective hitting technique as early as possible because this aids both accuracy and power. But probably the most important reason for establishing proper striking technique is safety. A neat and compact backswing, downswing and follow through on both sides of the court will minimise the chances of hitting your opponent with the racket.

Forehand

The backswing is the preparation of the stroke and will vary depending on the type of shot that you wish to play. Always take the racket back along the same path, with the wrist cocked at the top of the backswing: this will maximise racket head speed which in turn generates power. Always arrive to play the ball with the backswing already prepared. If you get there with the racket head down it is too late because there is seldom time to prepare suffici-

▲ *Cocked-wrist back lift:* left – *forehand;* right – *backhand*

ently at this split moment. The backswing should be prepared with the elbow slightly bent and the racket head pushed upwards. The wrist should be kept cocked: contrary to belief, most squash strokes should be performed with a firm wrist rather than with a flick of the wrist.

The racket head is then swung towards the ball, with an opening action at the elbow so that at the point of impact the arm is fully extended. Once again, the wrist should be kept cocked and the racket face should be open. (If you wish to play a straight drive on the forehand side – one of the most common strokes – then this is the correct swing to use.)

The final phase of the stroke is the follow through. For a right-handed player, the racket head should finish past your left ear, with the elbow bent.

▲ Basic forehand stroke ▶

◀ Keep the racket head up

Backhand

The backhand stroke really begins from where we left off with the forehand, i.e. from the forehand follow through. Unfold the arm from the elbow and then bring it down. Stay sufficiently far away from the ball that at the point of impact of the racket head with the ball the arm is fully extended. (For a drive this should be just in front of the leading foot.) Remember to keep the wrist cocked throughout the stroke. After impact, follow through so that the racket finishes in a high position.

When following through from a backhand try not to finish with the racket arm straight. Follow through upwards rather than outwards because the latter can be dangerous to the opponent and risk penalty at an advanced competitive level.

Top class players obtain their power from an effective backswing preparation, keeping the wrist cocked and transferring the weight from the back to the front foot and then on to the ball on impact. Good squash players do not normally generate power from pure physical strength.

▲ *Basic backhand stroke* ▶

Striking the ball

Basically, there are three positions from which you can take the ball in relationship to your leading foot (i.e. the left foot on the right-hand side of the court and the right foot on the left-hand side of the court – this is easily remembered as the foot nearer the front wall when facing the nearer side wall).

● **In front of the leading foot.** This position makes it easier to strike the ball from one side of the court to the other, i.e. to play a cross drive, cross lob or cross drop shot.

● **In line with the leading foot.** This is a very important position as it is used to hit the ball straight down the side walls, i.e. a straight drive from the front or back, straight volley, straight drop shots.

● **Behind the leading foot – 'taking the ball late'.** This position is used when you need to hit the side walls before the front wall, i.e. a boast out of the back corners, short angled shots at the front of the court. This position is very commonly used to aid disguise.

There are also three different moments when you will take the ball in relationship to its bounce off the floor.

● **Taking the ball on the rise.** This means that you speed up the game by moving on to the ball and taking it early, thus hurrying your opponent.

● **At the top of the bounce.** This is the most common time to hit the ball as it is at its slowest and therefore at its easiest to hit. Don't 'crowd' the ball.

● **On the fall or late.** This is used out of necessity if you have arrived late, or as a means of committing your opponent by delaying your shot.

Keeping the racket head up

When you are waiting for your opponent to strike the ball, the head of your racket should be 'up' and the racket across your body in front of you.

When you take your racket back before a forehand or a backhand stroke, the wrist should be cocked so that the head of your racket will be 'up'.

Always aim to keep the head of your racket as far 'up' as you can when you strike the ball. To put this another way: always aim to keep the head of the racket 'up' relative to the direction of your forearm, as this is the strongest position of the wrist.

Keep the racket head up and across ▶
your body in front of you

Taking the ball off the back wall

When taking the ball off the back wall, you must turn your body to face one of three positions.

- The side wall.
- The corner.
- The back wall.

With your racket prepared to strike the ball, remember to keep a comfortable distance away from both the wall and the back corner.

If you study the photographs, you will be able to see the correct positions of the feet and the body for such strokes.

A player need never be beaten except by the ball that drops really dead or clings to the back wall.

Use the side walls to get up the most difficult ones and hit upwards and hit hard.

▲ *Playing off the back wall, up the* ▶
nearer side wall

The two regular returns for balls coming off the back wall are:

- a straight return down the nearer side wall to a length. If possible, this is the best return to make and is governed by the degree of rebound that the ball makes off the back wall
- a 'boast'. This is a common return from the back corners, particularly useful for beginners. It is best used if you feel you cannot return the ball straight. The technique is to hit under the ball, lifting it upwards on to the side wall, making an angle which will carry the ball from the side wall on to the front wall in the opposite front corner.

◀ *Forehand boast*

Do not boast the ball unnecessarily, as it is apt to give your opponent an easy shot in the front of the court, but do not try to play the straight return down the side wall if there is any danger of hitting the back wall with your racket as you play the shot.

A ball that hits the back wall fairly hard and rebounds well clear of it may give an opening for a wide range of shots, such as the drop shot to either front corner or the reverse angle.

It is not always necessary to be on the defensive when your opponent's shot goes to the back of the court.

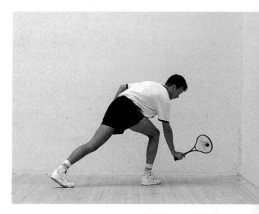

Backhand boast ▶

The service

The lob service is the best, provided the height of the court roof allows. It should be played from the front corner of the service box near the wall, and hit upwards on to the front wall, striking it about the centre of the area between the cut line and out of court line. The ball should continue upwards and strike the further side wall just below the out of court line, some three-quarters of the way down the court; and bounce on the floor before striking the back wall. A low, hard serve can be used for variety should the court have a low roof.

An alternative from the right-hand service box is the backhand serve. For this, strike the ball as close to the centre of the court as possible, so that it hits the front wall three-quarters of the way across and only a metre or so (a few feet) above the cut line, with the aim of bringing the ball back close to the opposite side wall to a good length.

▲ *Lob serve on the forehand*

22

▲ *Lob serve on the backhand* ▶

▲ *Low, hard serve on the forehand*

▲ *Low, hard serve on the backhand*

Return of service

The receiver of service must give himself the best possible chance of returning his opponent's service by being positioned in the opposite back half of the court. There are no rules governing where the receiver should stand, but you are advised to locate yourself somewhere in the region shown in fig. 10. This position does depend on the height and reach of the receiver.

In theory, the receiver should position himself in such a way that by just turning and taking one step he can reach the back wall with his racket, he can step forwards and volley the service, and by stepping backwards he can return a service which is played at him or down the middle of the court.

Obviously, an exact location cannot be specified since this very much depends on whether the player is a junior or a tall adult. One important point to remember from the outset is that it is advisable to get into the habit of returning forehand shots in the forehand side of the court, and also to return backhand shots in the backhand court. A common mistake with many beginners, they tend to turn in an attempt to play forehands in place of backhands. Playing a forehand return in the backhand court results in the player's back facing the side wall and this is not good technique. If you feel

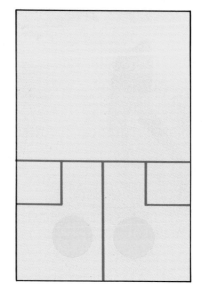

▲ *Fig. 10 Suggested positions when waiting to receive serve*

that your opponent's service is going to fall to a good length, it is better to volley the return, remembering to avoid:

● hitting the ball too hard – just push the racket face through the ball
● hitting it in a downwards direction unless it is a poor quality service which you can attack. The best defensive returns of a good service are either a straight return to a length along the side wall, or a cross court return to a length, taking care to play the ball over your opponent's head and not presenting him with an easy volley. This return can be dangerous because if the server is a good volleyer he can kill an inaccurate shot with a volley just above the tin. Therefore, practise a slow high-length return over the server's head as he stands in the centre court position. The striker can play a volley just above the tin in the front corner nearer to him.

By concentrating only on these three returns of service you will, with patience, develop accuracy.

One final hint: you should volley the service as much as you can.

Drop shot

There are three different types of drop shot that you can choose to play:

- straight
- angled (commonly used by top professionals)
- cross court.

There are several different techniques for hitting drop shots. They can be 'cut' or 'pushed', depending on your skill and the effect that you desire on the ball.

In terms of the stroke, the most important element is to keep the racket face open as shown in the photographs on pages 29 and 30. It is not necessary to take a long backswing but it *is* important to follow through, pushing the racket head in the direction you wish the ball to go. If you intend to cut the ball, then a certain degree of backswing is necessary to give the racket head a little momentum as it cuts across the underside of the ball. Keep the wrist firm so that the racket head follows the path of your hand.

Other important points to remember are:

- take the ball on the rise or at the top of its bounce
- set your feet along the line of the target to which you wish the ball to go
- remember to allow your opponent access to your shot after you have played it.

The best positions from which to play the drop shot are shown in fig. 11. Most effective are the positions shown in front of the 'T', although shots from further back may succeed against a slow opponent or one who watches the front wall instead of the ball.

You generally aim for a 'nick' with your drop shot and you should hit the ball as softly as you can. (The 'nick' is the point where the side walls join the floor. A ball landing in this spot rebounds unpredictably and very often hardly bounces at all.) When a drop shot is played from the front of the court it is essential to move away after completing the stroke to enable your opponent to have a clear view of the ball and to be able to strike it (fig. 12).

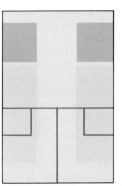 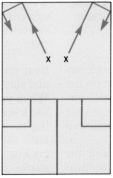 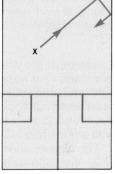

▲ *Fig. 11* Left *Straight drop shot (target area – red; area from which shot should be played – blue.* Middle *Angled drop shots.* Right *Cross court drop shots*

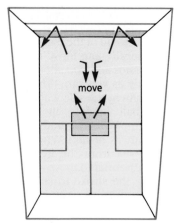

▲ Fig. 12 *After a drop shot is played in the front of the court, move away to allow your opponent a fair view*

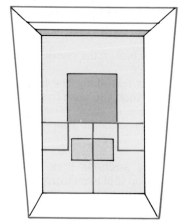

▲ Fig. 13 *When the ball is dropping in the red sector, your opponent will usually be somewhere in the blue sector; play a drop shot*

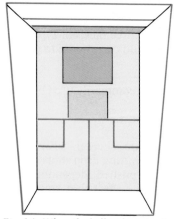

▲ Fig. 14 *When the ball is dropping further up the court (red sector) your opponent will usually be in the blue sector; play a hard-hit drive to the back of the court*

You must get your left foot well forward and your body well down on the forehand, and your right foot well forward and your body well down on the backhand. Reverse these instructions if you are left-handed.

The best method of practising the drop shot is to start close to the front wall near the centre of the court. Tap the ball gently on to the front wall and

then position yourself for the stroke and play it into one of the front corners. When you are satisfied that your footwork is correct and that you are striking the ball correctly, both early and late, then move further and further back in the court until you can play the stroke on to the front wall low down and softly from positions level with the service boxes.

Never play a drop shot unless your opponent is behind you, i.e. he must be further back in the court than you are when you strike the ball (figs 13 and 14), except for the surprise drop shot from the back of the court off the bad length shot.

To deceive your opponent, take your racket well back before playing the drop shot. This causes a doubt in the

▲ 'Cut' drop shot on the forehand

mind of your opponent because, if you swing your racket well back, he does not know if a drop shot is about to be played or whether you intend to hit the ball hard to the back of the court, and indeed you can do this at the last moment if you hear him coming up the court having anticipated a drop shot.

The backswing of the racket for the drop shot and for all strokes played in the forecourt are shown in the photographs on this page and page 30.

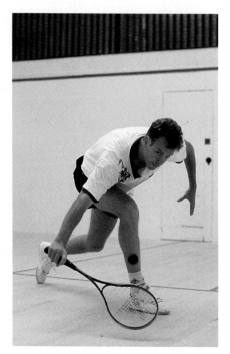

▲ *'Pushed' drop shot on the backhand*

Tactical considerations

You can usually tell when your opponent is about to play the drop shot, for he generally places one foot well forward and he crouches a little. Similarly, your opponent knows when you are going to play your drop shot. It follows therefore that, except when you play the perfect stroke, your opponent will be able to reach your drop. Now if you play a number of drops you will find that every time you gain a position in front of your opponent he will expect you to play one. Therefore, you will have enticed him up the court, close behind you as you play the stroke. Now, with your full backswing of the racket, you can either hit the ball hard to the back of the court or lob it gently to the back of the court, whichever you please.

Another method of playing the drop shot is to keep very upright as you approach the ball, making it appear that you are going to hit the ball to the back of the court. At the last second you bend down or crouch and play a drop shot. This is very difficult and needs perfect timing and a great deal of practice. You must watch the ball very closely. The photograph on the right shows the position when the ball is only 2 m (6 ft) away from the player. Could his opponent tell that a drop is about to be played?

*Can this player's opponent tell ▶
that a drop is about to be played?*

Angle shot

The angle shot is one that hits first the side wall and then the front wall. In most cases the ball should be hit hard.

When you strike the ball on the forehand, the left foot is as usual placed well forward and the left shoulder is well round towards the side wall. Similarly, when you strike the ball on the backhand, the right foot is well forward and the right shoulder is well round, pointing at the side wall.

Many players strike the ball very late, well after it has reached the top of its bounce. The best players, when they make winners, play the ball a few centimetres from the ground and yet, in the rallies, they often take the ball earlier, before the top of its bounce. This is in order to speed up the game, to make their opponents run and so to tire them. It is indeed most exhausting to be made to move up and down the court. It is far less tiring to run from side to side.

The best positions for the angle shots are shown in figs 15 and 16.

The reverse angle stroke is one played on to the opposite side wall

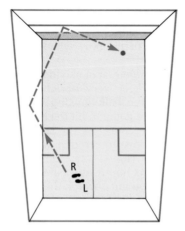

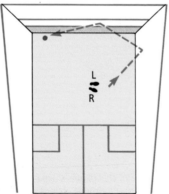

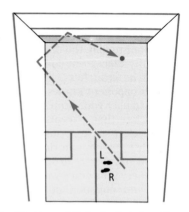

Fig. 15 Above left *Angle shot played from deep back in the court (backhand)*

Fig. 16 Below left *Angle shot played from in front of the centre line (forehand)*

Fig. 17 Above *Reverse angle shot on the forehand*

(fig. 17). If played very occasionally it may be a winning stroke, but it is difficult to play accurately.

Do not play the angle shot unless your opponent is either behind or level with you. The only exception to this is when your opponent is moving from the front of the court towards the centre court position: then you can play an angle or a drop shot. Very often you will catch him on the wrong foot.

A match between two really good players may well last up to two hours. The best way for you to tire your opponent is to make him move up and down the court; the best method of doing this is by means of the angle shot. Practise taking the angle shot on the rise and early, because this speeds up the game and your opponent is made to move faster up the court.

Tactical considerations

Masking your strokes is a very important factor in squash. A player often finds himself playing a stroke on his forehand from a position fairly far back in the court.

The position in the court and the stroke for tactical plan one are shown in fig. 18.

The usual stroke in this case is to hit the ball up the forehand side wall and back into the back corner. Now if you place your shoulder further round towards the side wall and make a full swing of the racket you can take the ball late, and play an angle shot. You must hit the ball hard and play it late.

Equally effective is the same stroke played from deep back in the court on the backhand.

Plan two is very similar, but the strokes are played in the front of the court.

During a rally you very often find yourself playing a stroke well up the court on the forehand. From this position you usually play either a drop shot or hit the ball hard to the back of the court.

The position in the court and the stroke for tactical plan two are shown in fig. 19.

Now by placing your left shoulder further round towards the side wall you can play this quick little angle shot, but you must take a full swing of the racket and play the ball late.

Equally effective is the same stroke played from well up the court on the backhand.

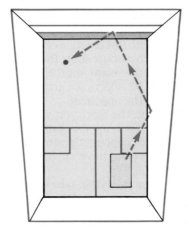

▲ Fig. 18 Tactical plan one

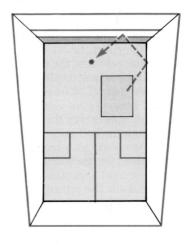

▲ Fig. 19 Tactical plan two

Volleying

Most of the top players look to volley the ball as much as possible because this has the effect of speeding up the game, and it also saves a good deal of running. If you are going to volley, then it is important to keep the racket 'up' at all times since this reduces the amount of time needed to hit the ball. Players who dangle or trail their racket tend not to be instinctive volleyers.

If you ever play against a person who trails his racket you should occasionally hit the ball hard down the centre of the court, i.e. at him as he stands in the centre of the court. You will find that you will be able to make quite a number of winners by this method. It is also a good idea to lift the ball because this makes the opponent delay playing the ball until it is in the back of the court, as a result of not being prepared for the volley.

One of the most important volleys to learn to make is the return of a good service. Do not allow the ball into the back corner, and apply the principles already mentioned in the section on the return of service.

Learn to look for volleys from around the centre of the court as shown in fig. 20. You have a choice of target from here by either volleying deep, which buries the opponent in the back corners, or by taking the ball short and low into the two front corners. Obviously the latter is more risky because the ball is being taken in just above the tin, but if played correctly this shot can be very profitable. These strokes are best played when the opponent is well out of position behind you.

Players with fast reactions can intercept poor cross court shots from as far forward as the point marked with a cross in fig. 20, applying a great deal of pressure on the opponent.

Remember, the more you volley the more you speed up the game, pressurising the opponent's strokes. To take volleys you have to think and work rapidly.

To practise volleying, take up a position around the centre of the court and from the wall feed yourself a ball between waist and head height at different distances from the wall. Then volley each ball either short into the front two corners, or deep into the back two corners.

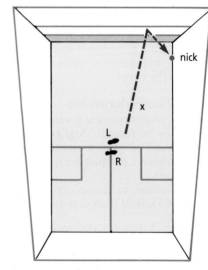

▲ Fig. 20 Volley from the centre of the court

▲ *Forehand volley*

▲ Backhand volley

Lobbing

This stroke can be one of the most important in the game, either in defence or attack. In defence it enables the striker to recover his position on the 'T' before his opponent can play his stroke, and in attack it can be devastating when played accurately and to a length, especially on a 'cold' court. The points to note are as follows.

● The ball can be lobbed from anywhere in the court.
● A good target is to get the ball out of your opponent's reach when on the 'T'.
● The ball will usually hit the front wall above the cut line. The only exception to this will be when the player is attempting a lob from a position close to the front wall. The usual position for the ball to hit the front wall is shown in fig. 21.
● The ball must pass over your opponent's head as he stands in the court.
● The lob is most effectively played across the court, and ideally should strike the side wall and then bounce on the floor to a good length. This type of lob makes your opponent play a defensive return because it is very risky to play a smash and if he lets it drop in the back corners it *should* be 'dying'.

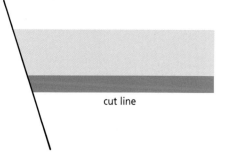

cut line

◀ *Fig. 21 Blue area indicates where the lob shot usually hits the front wall*

▲ *Forehand lob*

▲ *Backhand lob*

Advice on play

Watch the ball

Watch the ball until your opponent strikes it and then immediately move off in the direction in which he has struck it. Good players can move quickly, with the help of experience and anticipation, to be in a good position to strike the return early. Many players make the mistake of watching the front wall.

Be quite sure that you are watching the ball right on to your opponent's racket. Ask a friend to stand in the court balcony and tell you whether you are really watching your opponent striking the ball and whether you are immediately moving off in the direction in which he has struck it.

Recover

The actual centre of the court is clearly marked by two red lines which meet there and is therefore known as the 'T'.

After striking your return from any position in the court, it is good practice

to move as quickly as possible back to the 'T', including following a service (many players merely serve and wait for the opponent's return).

Always remember to watch the ball. If it is behind you, turn your head and feet towards the ball. You should be on

your toes and ready to move off in the direction of your opponent's return.

Hit to a length

This is one of the most important factors in playing squash well. Most good players base their game around hitting to a length.

All courts play differently depending on temperature and the materials used in construction. During the knock-up and first game try to establish a good length.

Basically, a good length ball is one that when hit to the back of the court 'dies' in the back corners. Length can be hit straight or across court, and can be hit hard as a drive or softly as a lob. A good general length to aim for is one bounce on the floor and then on to the back wall. This makes it difficult for the opponent to play successfully because for many players the back two corners are hard to return the ball from.

As already mentioned, you can hit the ball either hard or soft to a length, but remember to hit it higher up the front wall when playing softly.

◀ *On the 'T'*

Hit the ball into the back corners

The foundation of the game is to go on hitting the ball up the side walls or across the court into the opposite corner until you get such a good length ball into the back corner that your opponent is in difficulties. If he is a very good player he will return this difficult ball, but not to a length, and then you are in an attacking position so that you can play a drop shot or an angle shot or some other stroke that may possibly win the point.

Very often, among the moderate club players and below, the difficult length ball into the back corner is a winner.

Do not be in too much of a hurry to attempt a winning stroke. Rather let it be your aim to hit the ball into the back corners until you can gain a winning position in the front half of the court.

Do not take up a position in which the head is facing the front wall because the tendency will be to look in the same direction. To watch your opponent strike the ball from this position is a most unnatural movement.

As soon as you have struck the ball, when returning the service of your opponent, move into the centre of the court. And, finally, whenever you strike the ball during a rally, rush for the centre court position as fast as you can. You *must* be there before your opponent strikes the ball. You must realise from this that it is essential to play a stroke which will cause your opponent to move from the 'T' and give you a clear path to it.

Change of pace

It is essential to try to vary the pace of play. This can be achieved by either hitting the ball hard or softly, by moving on to the ball quickly or taking your time to hit it when allowed, and by taking the ball early by volleying.

Too many club players hit the ball too hard too often. This is a reasonable tactic if your opponent cannot cope with it, but if they can you need to change the pace to break up the rhythm of their play.

A very common error is not using the front wall to its best advantage. Many games are played in which the ball is consistently hit below the cut line. Try slowing the rallies down by lifting the ball high on the front wall. Playing this way is not as easy as it sounds if your opponent is experienced, and he may well be trying to do the same thing. Then it comes down to the accuracy of your stroke play and your mental toughness.

Attack and defence

All the best players make remarkably few mistakes. They play 'perfect' shots close to the tin only when they have plenty of time to make the strokes. They realise that by speed about the court and anticipation it is possible to return almost everything. They know that it is unwise to try anything spectacular. It almost seems as if every shot that they play comes either under the heading of a defensive stroke or an attacking one. An attacking stroke would mean a stroke to a length or an attempt at a 'perfect' drop or an angle shot played early or very late. A defensive stroke would mean getting the ball up in such a way as to give the player time to get to the centre of the court, before his opponent has time to strike the ball.

Stop yourself from trying to make attacking strokes from difficult positions and so avoid making too many errors. To do this get into the habit of saying to yourself as you run for every stroke 'Attack' if you consider that it is going to be an easy shot, or 'Defence' if you realise it is going to be a difficult return. After a time you will find that this process is becoming automatic and resulting in fewer mistakes.

Don't forget that the best defensive stroke is a high one hit slowly. This gives you time to reach the centre of the court. Then, wherever your opponent may hit the ball, you will have a chance to return it.

The pattern of a rally

Most club players and very many higher standard players lack continued concentration. They play well for a few minutes and then they make a succession of foolish mistakes, due entirely to lack of concentration.

You should learn to concentrate throughout every rally if possible. Following the end of the rally, try to relax and then focus on the next one rather than dwell on the success or failure of the preceding rally. Some players tend to worry about the previous point during the current rally, a practice that is irrelevant and costly; concentrate on the future.

Aim to make every rally a long one, unless you are presented with the opportunity to finish it off early from your opponent's poor shot.

Don't attempt to play a winning shot every time you strike the ball. This is a mistake of many club standard players. If the ball is hit well by your opponent and kept tight to the walls, or if he has you off balance, then merely return the ball and try once again to get it tight in an effort to create an opening.

The danger area

The danger area is that territory in which if you leave the ball you should expect an attacking shot from your opponent. The opponent can take the ball into the front of the court – either directly with effective drop shots or with side wall shots – or he can increase the pressure by playing hard cross court shots or straight lengths.

The danger area is that middle part of the court shown in fig. 22. Remember that the danger area is not the place to leave the ball.

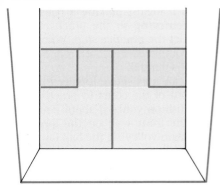

▲ *Fig. 22 Danger area*

Solo practice

If you find yourself on court alone, either because your opponent has not turned up or because you have arrived early, what can you do that will be of benefit to your game? Do you just knock the ball up and down the wall until you are bored enough to stop, or do you need a set pattern to work to?

Solo practice is far from boring if you have a constructive pattern in mind. It can be really hard work depending on how much effort you are willing to put into it. Many club players would probably not choose to practise alone, but for the top professionals solo practice is a very important part of their squash schedule.

Solo practice makes more sense if the session is divided into phases.

Phase 1

Warm up properly with a little stretching and then build up body heat with some slow all-court ghosting (simulating squash movements with no ball) for 2 or 3 minutes. After this you will probably find that you are more alert and ready to practise hard.

Phase 2

Now that you are warm you must get the ball warm. On your forehand side choose one of these target areas: either between the side wall and the outside line of the service box (the 'tramline') or anywhere within the forehand side of the court. Your own standard will help you make the choice. Keeping strictly on the forehand, try hitting this target area say 50 times consecutively without a mistake. If you should hit the ball off course or on the backhand, then start again from scratch until you achieve your goal. 50 is just an example and you should always set your own number, making sure that it is realistic but also a challenge.

For those players with quite good ball control, it is suggested that when you make a mistake you must recover the ball to the target area before it bounces more than twice, thus keeping the ball in continuous play and making you work harder.

Once you have achieved your target on the forehand, repeat the exercise on the backhand. You may wish to alter the target area or the number of consecutive hits depending on which is your stronger side.

Phase 3

This phase will help to improve your ball control even more. The target area now needs to be anywhere in the service box. Set yourself a number as a goal (5–15 to start). Begin on your forehand and hit the ball so that it lands in the target area for your set number. If you should hit too short or too long, don't stop – just correct the length, sticking to the one-bounce rule, and start from scratch until the number of consecutive hits is achieved. As before, repeat on the other side.

The next exercise is considerably harder. Hit the ball to such a length down the side wall that it bounces once on to the back wall and is then returned to do the same again. This can be termed 'hitting length to length'. This exercise requires excellent timing of the swing in the back of the court and good use of the face of the racket in order to get under the ball to lift it high (above the cut line) on to the front wall so that it returns to a good length. Once again set yourself a target number, somewhere between 3 and 30 depending on your standard. Initially set a conservative target because it is difficult to repeat the shot successfully early on. It is a help to use either a blue or red spot ball at this stage. Once again try to correct any mistakes without stopping, even if it means playing a boast and then retrieving to the practice area. Never let the practice stop. When you have completed the forehand, change to the backhand.

We can now move further towards the front of the court to practise volleys. Position yourself about 2 m (6 ft) from the front wall on the forehand side. Begin volleying the ball on to the front wall at a reasonably fast rate, attempting to keep the wrist firm and the racket face open to hit slightly underneath the ball. Using only a short backswing, punch the ball on to the

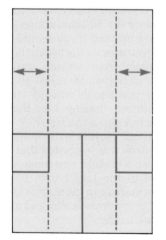

▲ *Fig. 23 Keep the ball within the tramlines*

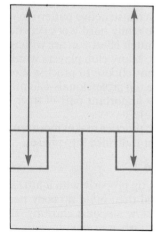

▲ *Fig. 24 Service boxes are the target*

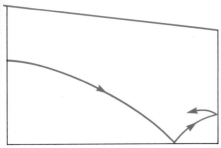

▲ Fig. 25 Hitting length to length

front wall. Now try to keep this going at a good pace for between 10 and 60 consecutive volleys without a mistake. Keep the ball in play and change to the backhand. When you do make a mistake, which is highly likely, only allow the ball to bounce once before retrieving it, and resume counting. Still without allowing the ball to hit the floor, move towards one of the front corners and volley on the forehand and backhand around the angle for your set number, making sure to stand a reasonable distance out and controlling the wrist from forehand to backhand.

Progress now on to the drop shot and angle practice. This is a difficult exercise to keep going because the idea is to practise finishing the shot off rather than playing ones which can be returned easily. It is suggested that you use a red or blue spot ball again here. Start off by playing forehand and backhand angle and reverse angle shots across the front of the court, using your imagination to decide which shot to play. As with all the other practices, do not allow the ball to bounce more than once, keeping the routine moving from angles to drops. Hit both straight angled and cross court shots off the bounce and on the volley, play the ball to all positions around the front of the court, and then play a drop but try to retrieve it and set yourself up with another from a different position. It would be better to set a time limit for this particular practice, say 4 minutes, and within that time count how many errors you make. Any more than two mistakes per minute is too many, so

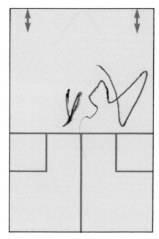

▲ Fig. 26 Short volleys

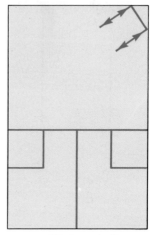

▲ Fig. 27 Corner volleys

45

over a period of 4 minutes try to make no more than eight mistakes. Don't count a winning shot as a mistake if you are unable to retrieve it – the mistakes are balls which end up in the tin.

To finish, try a combination of shots on the volley if you feel you are good enough, or alternatively off the bounce. Start close to the front wall on the forehand side and over 20 strokes lengthen the hit until you have moved back past the short line, keeping the ball under control. When you have achieved 20 consecutive shots without stopping, change to the backhand and gradually move forwards until you are once again close to the front wall after another 20 shots. Keeping the ball in play, move to the centre of the front wall and play 20 forehand to backhand angles across the body, and finally try 20 figure-of-eight shots, i.e. forehand across the body to hit the front wall, side wall and return across the body to hit the opposite corner, front wall, side wall, as shown in fig. 30.

By this time, if you have set reasonable targets you will have completed a solo practice of about 30–40 minutes. If you find yourself with only 10 minutes to spare, then merely attempt one of the sections separately.

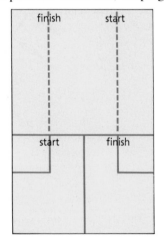

▲ *Fig. 28 Combination: up and down*

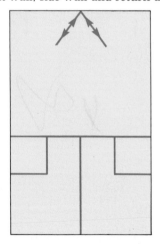

▲ *Fig. 29 Forehand to backhand angles*

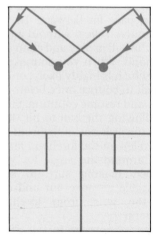

▲ *Fig. 30 Figure-of-eight shots*

Doubles

Squash doubles involves two teams of two playing against each other on the same court. Doubles courts are the same length as singles courts but are 1200 mm (approx. 4 ft 8 in) wider. There are very few wider courts any-where in the world, so most players who enjoy doubles play on singles courts.

In essence, the game is the same as singles. However, each pairing plays alternate strokes with the opposition. There is no requirement for the pair to alternate with each other, as they would in table tennis for example. While there are a few variations on singles squash – notably the scoring which is a point-a-rally up to 15 – the only other major difference is a rule by which many more points are played as lets. This is primarily for safety reasons – with four players swinging rackets in a comparatively small space, it is important to minimise the risk of players hitting each other with racket or ball.

Index